Fantastic 3-Ingredient Recipes

Quick and Easy Family Meals for Super Moms

BY

Stephanie Sharp

License Notes

My deepest thanks for buying my book! Now that you have made this investment in time and money, you are now eligible for free e-books on a weekly basis! Once you subscribe by filling in the box below with your email address, you will start to receive free and discounted book offers for unique and informative books. There is nothing more to do! A reminder email will be sent to you a few days before the promotion expires so you will never have to worry about missing out on this amazing deal. Enter your email address below to get started. Thanks again for your purchase!

Just visit the link or scan QR-code to get started!

https://stephanie-sharp.subscribemenow.com

Table of Contents

Introduction

Great meals may come in simple packages. That's what we are out to prove in bringing you this cookbook of 3-ingredient meals (discounting the constants like oil, salt, and pepper). The dishes featured here range from breakfast recipes to main course meals, soups, desserts, and snacks. This is so you can pull out something whenever you need help in the kitchen. You shouldn't always resort to fast food meals, you know!

We promise to give you some brilliant ideas on what to prepare when you are pressed for time and have limited stocks of supplies in the pantry. These recipe ideas are perfect for insanely busy days when you simply can't manage to squeeze in time for an elaborate dish yet you still want to please your family as they approach the dining table. With fewer ingredients, the demand for your time and effort is significantly reduced as well. So, what are you waiting for? Check out our collection of fantastic 3-ingredient meals and get excited which one to do first.

The 'Main' List:

- Easy Chicken Casserole
- Steak and Parmesan Potatoes
- Italian Pork Chops
- Mac and Cheese
- Spiced Chicken Wings
- Salsa Rice
- Sausage and Cabbage Casserole
- Quinoa and Chicken Thighs
- Dijon Pork Chops
- Quick & Easy Breakfast Skillet
- Roasted Vegetable Dinner
- Cajun Baby Back Ribs
- BBQ Meatball Hoagies
- Lemony Salmon Roast
- Sautéed Spinach

Snacks Attack:

- Tomato and Mozzarella Tarts
- Bacon-Wrapped Corn-on-the-Cob
- Tasty Zucchini Salad
- Chicken Avocado Salad
- Mini Egg Sliders
- Smoked Mozzarella Sticks
- Mini Tuna Peppers
- Bacon Egg Cups

The Dessert Honor Roll:

- Refreshing Watermelon Granita
- Chocolate Mousse
- Mud Pie
- Fruity Tart
- Peppermint Rocky Road Candies
- Chocolate Truffles
- Coconut Macaroons

These quick and easy recipes are proof that not all tasty meals require too much time and effort to make. You can create a hefty dinner even if your fridge seems empty. What's more, you can lend just a part of you in concocting those super quick and simple recipes so you can still keep up with your other duties in the household. This our way of saying, you can do it, super mom! Strut in style, in the kitchen and beyond.

The 'Main' List

Easy Chicken Casserole

Chicken is one of the easiest to prepare with very little ingredients because it is as delightful as it is. In this recipe, you only need some potatoes and cream of chicken soup to make a scrumptious dinner for the family. It's a great start for newbies in the kitchen because it cooks pretty quick. For seasoned cooks, they will find the basic recipe a great opportunity to become creative.

Serving Size: 4

Prep Time: 30 mins

Ingredients:

- 1 whole rotisserie chicken, deboned and chopped
- 1-14.5oz can cream of chicken soup
- 4 pcs potatoes, rinsed and thinly sliced

Instructions:

1. Preheat the oven to 350 degrees F. Prepare a lightly greased baking dish.
2. Heat cream of chicken soup in a pan over medium fire.
3. Add chopped chicken and boil. If the mixture is too thick, add some water.
4. Transfer chicken mixture into prepared baking dish.
5. Cover top with sliced potatoes.
6. Bake until potatoes are tender, about 30 minutes.

Steak and Parmesan Potatoes

Craving for a steak dinner? No problem. This recipe even comes with a crispy Parmesan potato side dish. And you only need three ingredients to make both. It's a complete meal in a plate. No, it's a delicious dinner in one serving. Your family will surely rave about this when you place it on the dining table.

Serving Size: 4

Prep Time: 1 hr.

Ingredients:

- 1 pc hanger steak (about 1 ½ lbs.)
- 2 lbs. new potatoes, rinsed
- ¾ cup Parmesan cheese, grated
- *½ cup olive oil, divided
- *Kosher salt and black pepper to taste

Instructions:

1. Boil the potatoes in a pot of salted water for about 14-15 minutes or until tender.
2. Arrange potatoes in a baking sheet to cool a little, then, crush lightly in between your palms.
3. Heat about 3 tablespoons of oil in an oven-safe skillet over medium fire.
4. Stir in the potatoes and brown. Sprinkle with some salt and cook for about 15 minutes.
5. Sprinkle browned potatoes with grated Parmesan and toss to combine. Cook for about 2 minutes or until cheese is crisp. Place in a platter and set aside.
6. Rub some salt and pepper onto steak.
7. Heat about 2 tablespoons of oil in another pan and pan-fry steak for about 6 minutes, turning once.
8. Allow steak to rest for about 5 minutes in a chopping board before slicing it across the grain.
9. Place on the platter with crispy Parmesan Potatoes.

Italian Pork Chops

Pork chops are made more charming with brown sugar and Italian dressing mix. It's a pretty basic flavoring that could make a lot of difference on the taste of your meat. Since this is oven roasted, you barely have a need for grease, making it super healthy. This is one of the best and easiest weeknight dinners you can pull off for the family. Pair it with some steamed veggies and you're good to go.

Serving Size: 8

Prep Time: 25 mins

Ingredients:

- 8 pcs boneless pork chops
- 1 small packet Italian Dressing Mix
- ½ cup brown sugar

Instructions:

1. Preheat the oven to 425 degrees F. Prepare a baking pan, lined with aluminum foil to make clean up a breeze.
2. Mix together Italian dressing mix and brown sugar.
3. Rub mixture generously onto pork chops and arrange in prepared pan
4. Bake on preheated oven for about 25 minutes, then, raise the temperature and broil for about 2 minutes, allowing the sugar to caramelize.
5. Serve and enjoy.

Mac and Cheese

A macaroni and cheese recipe does not always have to be elaborate. Sometimes, the simplest could be the tastiest. This recipe is proof. It's creamy and delicious and super fast to make. Since mac and cheese has been elected as kid's favorite, you can offer this to your kids any mealtime and for sure, they will love it.

Serving Size: 3

Prep Time: 20 mins

Ingredients:

- 1 lb. elbow macaroni
- 2 cups cheddar cheese, shredded
- 5 cups milk

Instructions:

1. Heat milk in a pot until it boils.
2. Stir in elbow macaroni and cook for about 10 minutes, stirring frequently.
3. Remove from heat and add shredded cheddar. Toss until cheese melts and coats the macaroni evenly.
4. Serve immediately.

Spiced Chicken Wings

Chicken wings are always a favorite meal for kids and adults alike. Next time you are serving this dish, try this 3-ingredient recipe, which will provide a different flavor to your meat, making it even more interesting to eat. Try this with a creamy ranch dressing and for sure, you will not be able to stop munching.

Serving Size: 4

Prep Time: 25 mins

Ingredients:

- 1 ½ lbs. chicken wings, cut into two
- 2 tsp Old Bay seasoning
- 3 tbsp unsalted butter, melted
- *1 tsp olive oil

Instructions:

1. Coat chicken wings evenly in oil and a teaspoon of Old Bay seasoning.
2. Preheat grill to medium fire.
3. Place chicken wings on the grill to cook, uncovered, turning once for about 15 minutes.
4. Combine remaining seasoning with butter in a large bowl.
5. Add hot-off-the-grill chicken wings and toss gently to coat.
6. Serve immediately with a creamy ranch dressing or any dip you desire.

Salsa Rice

If you have been growing bored with your regular rice meals, try this recipe. It will give you a different perspective on the meal altogether with some spicy Mexican seasoning. Of course, you have the power to up the spiciness level or tone it down, depending on who you are serving this to. But regardless, this is a yummy way to have rice, whether for lunch or dinner.

Serving Size: 5

Prep Time: 15 mins

Ingredients:

- 2 cups instant rice
- 1 ½ cups salsa
- 1 ½ cups Monterey Jack cheese, shredded
- *1 ½ cups water

Instructions:

1. Combine water and salsa in a pan until blended. Heat over medium fire and boil.
2. Add rice, then, turn off heat. Cover the pan and let the dish sit for about 5 minutes.
3. Stir in cheese to melt. Serve immediately.

Sausage and Cabbage Casserole

A casserole is always a welcome dish to any household. And for super moms, who works hard to make sure their family eat vegetables at all cost, this Sausage and Cabbage Casserole is a witty idea. Never mind the fact that it only requires 3 ingredients to make. It is super delicious and healthy and that's enough reason for you to make this one day.

Serving Size: 6

Prep Time: 3 hrs.

Ingredients:

- 4 lbs. cabbage, cored, shredded, and blanched
- 2 lbs. sweet Italian pork sausage, casings removed
- 3 tbsp unsalted butter
- *Salt and black pepper to taste

Instructions:

1. Preheat the oven to 300 degrees F. Prepare a baking dish, greased with butter.
2. Layer cabbage and sausage crumbles on prepared pan, ending with cabbage.
3. Place remaining butter on top of the dish, cover tightly with parchment paper, then, with aluminum foil.
4. Bake for 2 hours, then, remove cover and bake for another half an hour.
5. Serve warm.

Quinoa and Chicken Thighs

Quinoa cooked in salsa verde is a great base for some tasty chicken thighs. This dinner dish is a go-to recipe when you need to serve something flavorful but you have less than an hour to spare. The jar of salsa verde also cuts the trip short from preparing too many other ingredients. It's fully packed with flavor and very tasty.

Serving Size: 4

Prep Time: 35 mins

Ingredients:

- 1 cup dry quinoa
- 4 pcs chicken thighs
- 1-15oz jar salsa verde
- *½ cup water
- *Freshly ground black pepper to taste

Instructions:

1. Preheat the oven to 400 degrees F.
2. Rub pepper all over chicken thighs, then, heat in an oven-safe skillet over medium fire to render chicken fat, about 5 minutes. Transfer chicken to a bowl and set aside.
3. In the same pan with chicken fat, sauté quinoa for 2 minutes.
4. Stir in salsa verde and water and boil, then reduce heat to low, place chicken thighs on top, and simmer for 5 minutes.
5. Place skillet in preheated oven and bake for 20 minutes until chicken is cooked through and the liquid is fully absorbed.

Dijon Pork Chops

Turn regular pork chops into an extravagant dinner dish for the family by adding a breadcrumbs coating. The trick for a no-fail outcome is to ensure you do not overcook the meat so it is still juicy and tender but is cooked through.

Serving Size: 6

Prep Time: 30 mins

Ingredients:

- 6 pcs boneless pork loin chops
- 3 tbsp Dijon mustard
- 1/3 cup seasoned breadcrumbs
- *Pinch of pepper
- Cooking spray

Instructions:

1. Preheat the oven to 375 degrees F. Prepare a lightly greased baking dish.
2. Combine breadcrumbs and pepper in a bowl, then, spread mustard onto pork chops.
3. Coat meat with breadcrumbs and arrange onto prepared baking dish.
4. Place in the oven and let the meat cook for 20 minutes, until a meat thermometer inserted on the meat reads 145 degrees F.
5. Let the meats rest for about 5 minutes before serving.

Quick & Easy Breakfast Skillet

This breakfast casserole is pretty versatile. You can serve it on its own for a complete breakfast meal or you can serve it with salad or steamed veggies for dinner. It's a very simple recipe that requires only three ingredients. The salsa has everything required to provide some body and deep flavor onto meat.

Serving Size: 4

Prep Time: 50 mins

Ingredients:

- 6 large eggs
- 6 cups of fresh pico de gallo, strained
- *Kosher salt and ground black pepper to taste
- 3 1/2 ounces of crumbled feta (about 3/4 cup)
- *1/3 cup olive oil

Instructions:

1. Preheat the oven to 375 degrees F.
2. Heat some oil in an oven-safe skillet over medium fire and sauté pico de gallo with some salt. Cook in a low simmer for 25 minutes.
3. Add feta cheese and then, crack the eggs carefully, one-by-one. Sprinkle with more salt and some pepper.
4. Turn off the heat and place skillet in preheated oven and cook for about 15 minutes.
5. Serve immediately.

Roasted Vegetable Dinner

Roasted veggies are a joy to have, especially when you want something refreshing for dinner. It's a good break from meats and greasy food, since it is super healthy and not to mention, delicious. The secret to making this recipe right is to learn the proper temperature that will keep them moist and tasty as they are roasting in the oven.

Serving Size: 4

Prep Time: 45 mins

Ingredients:

- 2 lbs. root vegetable mix, peeled and cubed (carrots, beets, potatoes, turnips, radishes, sweet potatoes)
- ½ cup olive oil
- 4 pcs eggs, fried, sunny side up style
- *Salt and pepper to taste

Instructions:

1. Preheat the oven to 425 degrees F.
2. Place veggies in a baking dish, drizzle with oil, and sprinkle with some salt and pepper.
3. Roast for about half an hour, stirring occasionally to keep the vegetables evenly cooked and browned
4. Serve with sunny side up eggs.

Cajun Baby Back Ribs

You don't need too much to make your baby back ribs taste delightful. That makes it a perfect feature in this 3-ingredient recipe book. As long as it is properly seasoned and roasted, you can expect a good meal out of it. You just have to be patient because having the best-tasting ribs also means cooking it slow. Let's get started.

Serving Size: 2

Prep Time: 2 hrs. 25 mins

Ingredients:

- ½ rack baby back ribs
- 1 cup BBQ sauce
- 3 tbsp Cajun seasoning

Instructions:

1. Preheat the oven to 250 degrees F.
2. Rub seasoning all over the ribs, then, place the rack in a baking dish and roast, covered with aluminum foil, for 2 hours.
3. Remove foil, increase heat to 500 degrees F, and coat the ribs evenly in BBQ sauce. Bake for 15 minutes more.
4. Allow to rest for 10 minutes before slicing and serving.

BBQ Meatball Hoagies

Meatballs can be bought frozen and you will only have to thaw them to enjoy this recipe. That makes this a simple meal that you can prepare quickly. This is a hit among kids and adults alike for its meaty goodness, and yes, the sweet and tangy BBQ sauce.

Serving Size: 4

Prep Time: 30 mins

Ingredients:

- 16 pcs frozen meatballs, thawed
- 1 pc refrigerated crusty French loaf
- ¾ cup barbecue sauce
- *Cooking spray

Instructions:

1. Preheat the oven to 350 degrees F. Prepare a lightly greased baking sheet. Set aside.
2. Cut French loaf to make 4 pieces of buns and place on prepared sheet, making sure they are 2 inches apart.
3. Bake for about 20 minutes until the buns are nicely golden.
4. Meanwhile, place meatballs and barbecue sauce in a pan and heat on low until heated through.
5. Cut buns with a slit in the middle and spoon over about 4 meatballs each.
6. Serve immediately.

Lemony Salmon Roast

If you are looking for a healthy food that your family will not put down and which you can cook with just a few ingredients, salmon makes for a wonderful choice. This Omega-3 loaded fish is also packed with yumminess. You don't have to do much with it other than roasting it with some lemon and basil leaves.

Serving Size: 4

Prep Time: 25 mins

Ingredients:

- 4 pcs salmon fillets
- 2 pcs lemons, thinly sliced, plus grated lemon peels
- 2 tbsp fresh basil, thinly sliced
- *2 tsp olive oil
- *Salt and pepper to taste

Instructions:

1. Preheat the oven to 375 degrees F. Prepare a baking sheet, lightly greased with some oil.
2. Place the salmon fillets, scatter grated lemon peel and basil leaves on top, then, drizzle with remaining oil.
3. Finally, season with salt and pepper before topping with lemon slices.
4. Bake for about 15 minutes until flaky and cooked through. Serve immediately.

Sautéed Spinach

Talking about simple, this sautéed spinach dish is super basic, you can make it even with your eyes closed. Since it has nothing more than garlic and onions, you can find a way to enhance it to match your taste, or even just to make use of whatever is available in your pantry. You can add meat, tofu, sauce, and other veggies. But believe it or not, you don't have to do all those to ensure you can serve something equally delicious

Serving Size: 4

Prep Time: 10 mins

Ingredients:

- 1 ½ lbs. fresh spinach, trimmed
- 1 garlic clove, peeled and minced
- 1 pc onion, chopped
- *2 tbsp olive oil
- *Salt and freshly ground pepper to taste

Instructions:

1. Heat oil in a pan over medium fire and sauté garlic and onions until fragrant.
2. Stir in spinach, season with salt and pepper, and increase heat on high to cook the spinach until wilted.
3. Serve immediately.

Snacks Attack

Tomato and Mozzarella Tarts

Looking for a simple recipe that you can serve your children as a snack? Here's a tasty tart that's worth the effort. All you need to prepare this recipe are tomatoes and cheese. It's a joyful snack recipe that will make your kids jump with happiness.

Serving Size: 4

Prep Time: 1 hr.

Ingredients:

- ½ sheet puff pastry
- 1 cup cherry tomatoes, halved
- 4 oz mozzarella cheese, grated
- *1 tbsp olive oil
- *Kosher salt and black pepper to taste

Instructions:

1. Preheat the oven to 425 degrees F. Prepare a baking sheet lined with parchment paper.
2. Dust your work surface with some flour, then, roll the pastry sheet in to a 9x6 rectangle. Arrange in prepared baking sheet and place in the fridge for 30 minutes or until firm.
3. When the pastry sheet is ready, prick the surface using fork.
4. Top with tomatoes and cover with cheese.
5. Drizzle tart with oil and season with salt and freshly ground black pepper.
6. Bake for 20 minutes until golden brown. Rest for 5 minutes before slicing and serving.

Bacon-Wrapped Corn-on-the-Cob

Corn on the cob is made even more delightful with a bacon wrap. After your first bite, you will surely be convinced that this is exactly how you do it, instead of the conventional way. Bacon fat is definitely a great alternative to a flavorful dot of butter. It's a great party idea next time you hold a backyard barbecue for friends and relatives.

Serving Size: 8

Prep Time: 30 mins

Ingredients:

- 8 pcs bacon strips
- 8 pcs sweet corn ears, husks removed
- 2 tbsp chili powder

Instructions:

1. Wrap each piece of bacon onto each sweet corn ear.
2. Place in a sheet of aluminum foil, sprinkle with some chili powder, and seal, twisting the ends securely.
3. Preheat grill on medium and grill corn for about 25 minutes.
4. Serve immediately.

Tasty Zucchini Salad

Zucchini is a delightful veggie that is suitable as a filling snack with only a few ingredients added in. This recipe is proof of how a simple roasted zucchini can turn into a meal if you toss it with some seasonings, the perfect treatment for most veggies during the summer season. Try it today!

Serving Size: 6

Prep Time: 12 mins

Ingredients:

- 2 pcs zucchini, trimmed and sliced
- 2 tbsp white wine vinegar
- 4 tbsp corn oil
- Salt and black pepper to taste

Instructions:

1. Preheat the oven to 400 degrees F.
2. Arrange zucchini slices in a baking sheet. Season with some salt and pepper.
3. Toast for about 5 minutes or until soft.
4. Transfer zucchini in a bowl, toss with vinegar and oil, and serve.

Chicken Avocado Salad

You won't believe it but this 3-ingredient meal is a winner for both health buffs super moms who want to get things done in a-breeze. You don't need much for this yummy Chicken Avocado Salad. All that you need is some leftover rotisserie chicken, avocado, and fresh cilantro. You can use it as a sandwich or pita bread filling, or eat it on its own, served on lettuce cups. From the basic recipe, you may add other ingredients as you like and as available, including onions, yogurt, garlic powder, or chopped nuts.

Serving Size: 4

Prep Time: 10 mins

Ingredients:

- 2 cups leftover rotisserie chicken, shredded
- 1 pc avocado, cored and chopped
- ¼ cup cilantro, chopped
- *Salt & pepper to taste

Instructions:

1. Combine all the ingredients in a bowl, mashing gently until combined. Season with salt and pepper and serve.

Mini Egg Sliders

Wondering what to serve alongside your favorite barbecue dishes? Here's an easy to prepare recipe that you can use and it could make your buffet spread perfect. We are 100% sure your guests and family alike will love this. After all, who can resist a real good egg salad recipe?

Serving Size: 8

Ingredients:

- 1-5oz can tuna, drained
- 8 pcs mini sweet peppers, halved and seeded
- 2 tbsp mayonnaise
- *Salt and pepper, to taste

Instructions:

1. Combine tuna and mayonnaise in a bowl. Season with salt and pepper and stir to blend.
2. Scoop into pepper halves and serve.

Bacon Egg Cups

Give your muffin cups something to work on other than a sweet dessert. This time, you can use them for a very satisfying egg snack, with bacon, mind you. This is a great treat for your kids after school, something they could look forward to.

Serving Size: 5

Prep Time: 35 mins

Ingredients:

- 5 pcs eggs
- 5 pcs bacon slices
- 1 tsp chives, chopped
- *Salt and pepper to taste

Instructions:

1. Preheat the oven to 400 degrees F.
2. Arrange a bacon strip to cover the bottom and the sides of each muffin cup, carefully crack an egg in the middle, sprinkle with chopped chives, salt, and pepper.
3. Bake for 15-20 minutes, depending on how well you want your eggs cooked.
4. Serve and enjoy.

The Dessert Honor Roll

Refreshing Watermelon Granita

Are you looking for a refreshing dessert that will add color to your already vibrant summer? This watermelon granita is a great choice for that. It's a cool and refreshingly sweet treat that wonderfully requires nothing more than just watermelon, sugar, and lemon juice.

Serving Size: 6

Prep Time: 2 hrs. 30 mins

Ingredients:

- 1 lb. watermelon, trimmed, cut into chunks, and frozen
- 2 tbsp lemon juice
- 2 tbsp sugar

Instructions:

1. Place frozen watermelon chunks, lemon juice, and sugar in a blender. Process until liquefied.
2. Transfer mixture in a ceramic pan and freeze for 2 hours or so, using a fork to break up the crystals often to create a slushy and crunchy dessert.

Chocolate Mousse

There is something about this Chocolate Mousse that will surely endear you to it. It is light, loaded with chocolatey goodness, and whips up quick and easy with only a few ingredients. You will never have a reason not to do this for yourself, especially since it could make you feel really good with a few spoonfuls or so.

Serving Size: 8

Prep Time: 8 hrs. 15 mins

Ingredients:

- 2 cups dark chocolate, roughly chopped
- 2 ¼ cups whipping cream
- 1 tsp vanilla extract

Instructions:

1. Heat cream in a pan over medium fire until it bubbles softly.
2. Stir in chocolates and whisk until chocolates are melted.
3. Add vanilla and stir until smooth.
4. Cool and place in the fridge until well chilled.
5. Whip cream in a mixer, continuously beating until stiff.
6. Transfer to a pipe and pour onto glasses and serve.

Mud Pie

A mud pie is a precious dessert that you can easily whip up with just three ingredients: ice cream, pie shell, and chocolates. It's hard to resist, since it is loaded with sweet chocolate goodness loaded into a pie. The best way to cut a slice into your mud pie is allowing a sharp blade to run under hot water and wipe dry before using.

Serving Size: 8

Prep Time: 1 hr. 40 mins

Ingredients:

- 1-9in frozen pie shell, slightly thawed
- 2 pints coffee ice cream
- 6oz semisweet chocolate, chopped and divided

Instructions:

1. Preheat the oven to 350 degrees F. Place pie shell in a pan and prick with a fork.
2. Bake for 25 minutes and set aside to cool.
3. Place chocolates in a double broiler, stirring continuously until smooth and melted.
4. Spread half of melted chocolate on the pie shell and freeze for 5 minutes or until firm.
5. Allow ice cream to soften, until spreadable, then, scoop onto prepared pie shell. Smoothen top and freeze for an hour.
6. Keep the remaining chocolate heated in the microwave until smooth. Drizzle on top of the pie and freeze again.
7. Slice and serve.

Fruity Tart

These Fruit Tarts will change the way you look at tarts. It's refreshingly sweet and will be ready in less than an hour. What's more, it only requires three ingredients, so you won't have to break your pantry along the way.

Serving Size: 6

Prep Time: 25 mins

Ingredients:

- 16oz fresh strawberries, sliced
- 1 sheet of frozen puff pastry, thawed
- 1 tbsp sugar

Instructions:

1. Preheat the oven to 400 degrees F.
2. Arrange the puff pastry sheet in a baking pan lined with parchment paper.
3. Place strawberry slices on top of the puff pastry, then, sprinkle with sugar.
4. Bake for 20 minutes until golden brown.

Peppermint Rocky Road Candies

These rocky road candies are very nice. They can be prepared ahead of time so your kids can bring them to school or just keep them in the fridge so you can have something to pull off anytime you need a quick dessert. The hint of peppermint makes the candies even more addictive.

Serving Size: 6

Prep Time: 50 mins

Ingredients:

- ¾ cup peppermint candies, crushed and divided
- 12oz dark chocolate, chopped
- 1 cup mini marshmallows

Instructions:

1. Melt chocolate in a double broiler, stirring constantly until smooth.
2. Fold in marshmallows and half of the crushed candies.
3. Drop mixture onto parchment paper lined baking sheets, sprinkle with remaining crushed candies. Place in the fridge to set.

Chocolate Truffles

Chocolate Truffles make for a nice dessert and since this recipe only need 3 ingredients, it's a quick and super easy dessert that you can whip up to delight your family. You will love this, promise. Your kids will keep begging for this.

Serving Size: 6

Prep Time: 45 mins

Ingredients:

- 8oz cream cheese
- 2 cups chocolate, chopped
- ½ cup candy sprinkles

Instructions:

1. Beat cream cheese and a cup of melted chocolate in an electric mixer until combined.
2. Scoop onto parchment paper lined baking sheets and place in the fridge to chill.
3. When the truffles have set, dip onto melted chocolate and candy sprinkles, and place back into the baking sheet.

Coconut Macaroons

Coconut macaroons, anyone? This is a fantastic recipe to follow with its simple steps and just three ingredients. You can whip up this dessert in only 10 minutes. Yes, you read that right. You only need 10 minutes to make delectable coconut macaroons for the family.

Serving Size: 6

Prep Time: 10 mins

Ingredients:

- 16oz unsweetened coconut flakes
- 1 can condensed milk
- ¼ tsp vanilla extract

Instructions:

1. Preheat the oven to 350 degrees F. Prepare a lightly greased baking sheet and set aside.
2. Mix together milk and coconut flakes.
3. Scoop them onto prepared baking sheets and bake for 8 minutes or until the top turns golden brown.

Conclusion

Don't we all love super quick and easy recipes that you can make even when your food pantry is almost empty? With these 3-ingredient recipes, preparing breakfast, lunch, dinner, and snacks and desserts in between will never be a problem. You can pull out any of these recipes any time you need to and be able to whip up a meal with only 3 ingredients.

These 3-ingredient meals are perfect for super busy moms who always have their hands full and yet, they are expected to be kitchen superstars who can instantly concoct delightful recipes. You can be that super mom that you want when you have this cookbook on the ready.

You will no longer have an excuse for concocting recipes that your family could love no matter how tough life is.

Happy cooking!

About the Author

Born in New Germantown, Pennsylvania, Stephanie Sharp received a Masters degree from Penn State in English Literature. Driven by her passion to create culinary masterpieces, she applied and was accepted to The International Culinary School of the Art Institute where she excelled in French cuisine. She has married her cooking skills with an aptitude for business by opening her own small cooking school where she teaches students of all ages.

Stephanie's talents extend to being an author as well and she has written over 400 e-books on the art of cooking and baking that include her most popular recipes.

Sharp has been fortunate enough to raise a family near her hometown in Pennsylvania where she, her husband and children live in a beautiful rustic house on an extensive piece of land. Her other passion is taking care of the furry members of her family which include 3 cats, 2 dogs and a potbelly pig named Wilbur.

Watch for more amazing books by Stephanie Sharp coming out in the next few months.

Author's Afterthoughts

I am truly grateful to you for taking the time to read my book. I cherish all of my readers! Thanks ever so much to each of my cherished readers for investing the time to read this book!

With so many options available to you, your choice to buy my book is an honour, so my heartfelt thanks at reading it from beginning to end!

I value your feedback, so please take a moment to submit an honest and open review on Amazon so I can get valuable insight into my readers' opinions and others can benefit from your experience.

Thank you for taking the time to review!

Stephanie Sharp

For announcements about new releases, please

follow my author page on Amazon.com!

(Look for the Follow Bottom under the photo)

You can find that at:

https://www.amazon.com/author/stephanie-sharp

*or Scan **QR-code** below.*

www.ingramcontent.com/pod-product-compliance
Lightning Source LLC
LaVergne TN
LVHW060348090625
813371LV00001B/9